Too Cute To Handle

SLEEPING CATS

A Heart-warming Photo Book for Cat Lovers, with Beautiful Quotes & Adorable Pictures of Feline Friends, Cats and Kittens. All in Sweet & Funny Sleepy Postures!

Odilia O. Jenkins

Copyright © 2016 by Odilia O. Jenkins

All right reserved. This book or any portion thereof may not be reproduced
or used in any manner whatsoever without the express written permission of the publisher,
except for the use of brief quotations in a book review.

"Authors like cats because they are such quiet, lovable, wise creatures, and cats like authors for the same reasons."

Robertson Davies

"Intelligence in the cat is underrated."

Louis Wain

"Cats know how to obtain food without labor, shelter without confinement, and love without penalties."

W. L. George

"Just watching my cats can make me happy."

Paula Cole

"Perhaps it is because cats do not live by human patterns, do not fit themselves into prescribed behavior, that they are so united to creative people."

Andre Norton

"Time spent with cats is never wasted."

Sigmund Freud

"You can not look at a sleeping cat and feel tense."

Jane Pauley

"There are two means of refuge from the miseries of life: music and cats."

Albert Schweitzer

"My relationships with my cats has saved me from a deadly, pervasive ignorance."

William S. Burroughs

"Cats are connoisseurs of comfort."

James Herriot

"I grew up with such an affinity to cats. I adore the way that they think and operate."

Guy Pearce

"A cat is a puzzle for which there is no solution."

Hazel Nicholson

"It is impossible for a lover of cats to banish these alert, gentle, and discriminating friends, who give us just enough of their regard and complaisance to make us hunger for more."

Agnes Repplier

"People meeting for the first time suddenly relax if they find they both have cats. And plunge into anecdote."

Charlotte Gray

"I'm not sure why I like cats so much.
I mean, they're really cute obviously. They are both wild
and domestic at the same time."

Michael Showalter

"I always looked up to so many people before me and was lucky to become such good friends with them. I learned so much hanging out with those cats."

Kid Rock

"What greater gift than the love of a cat?"

Charles Dickens

"Cats are rather delicate creatures and they are subject to a good many different ailments, but I have never heard of one who suffered from insomnia."

Joseph Wood Krutch

Thank you for your purchase of this book. I hope you find it enjoyable! You can let me know what you think by posting a review on an amazon website.

Your reviews are valuable to those who adore these wonderful feline friends like we do. I thank you so much again for your continuous support!

Odilia O. Jenkins

Printed in Great Britain
by Amazon